# Immigration to the United States

# Russian Immigrants

*Lisa Trumbauer*

*Robert Asher, Ph.D., General Editor*

☑® Facts On File, Inc.

**Immigration to the United States: Russian Immigrants**

Facts On File, Inc.
132 West 31st Street
New York NY 10001

**Library of Congress Cataloging-in-Publication Data**

Trumbauer, Lisa, 1963-
  Russian immigrants / Lisa Trumbauer.
    p. cm. – (Immigration to the United States)
  Includes bibliographical references and index.
  ISBN 0-8160-5685-4
  1. Russian Americans–History–Juvenile literature. 2. Immigrants–United States–History–Juvenile literature. 3. Russian Americans–Juvenile literature. I. Title. II. Series.
  E184.R9T78 2004
  973'.049171–dc22

2004017853

Facts On File books are available at special discounts when purchased in bulk quantities for businesses, associations, institutions, or sales promotions. Please call our Special Sales Department in New York at (212) 967-8800 or (800) 322-8755.

You can find Facts On File on the World Wide Web at http://www.factsonfile.com

Cover design by Cathy Rincon
A Creative Media Applications Production
Interior design: Fabia Wargin & Luís Leon
Editor: Laura Walsh
Copy editor: Laurie Lieb
Proofreader: Tania Bissell
Photo researcher: Jennifer Bright

Photo Credits:
p. 1 © Bettmann/CORBIS; p. 4 © CORBIS; p. 11 © CORBIS; p. 15 © Getty Images/Hulton Archive; p. 17 © Bettmann/CORBIS; p. 19 © CORBIS; p. 23 © The Granger Collection, New York; p. 25 © CORBIS; p. 26 © The Granger Collection, New York; p. 30 © The Granger Collection, New York; p. 31 © Getty Images/Hulton Archive; p. 35 © Minnesota Historical Society/CORBIS; p. 37 Courtesy Ellis Island Museum; p. 40 © North Wind Archives; p. 43 © Bettmann/CORBIS; p. 47 © Bettmann/CORBIS; p. 52 © Bettmann/CORBIS; p. 53 © Baldwin H. Ward & Kathryn C. Ward/CORBIS; p. 55 © Getty Images/Hulton Archive; p. 57 © Getty Images/Hulton Archive; p. 60 © CORBIS; p. 63 © The Granger Collection, New York; p. 65 © AP Photo; p. 67 © Bettmann/CORBIS; p. 69 © David Rubinger/CORBIS; p. 72 © AP Photo; p. 75 © Bettmann/CORBIS; p. 78 © Bettmann/CORBIS; p. 81 © AP Photo/Peter Morgan; p. 83 © AP Photo; p. 86 © Mark Peterson/CORBIS.

Printed in the United States of America

VH PKG 10 9 8 7 6 5 4 3 2 1

This book is printed on acid-free paper.

Previous page: *First Lady Eleanor Roosevelt welcomes recent Russian immigrant children to the United States in 1943.*

# Contents

# Preface to the Series

# A Nation
# of Immigrants

*Robert Asher, Ph.D.*

*Left: A Russian family poses for a portrait as they arrive at Ellis Island aboard the* Orbita *in 1921. The immigration processing facility on Ellis Island in New York Harbor was the first stop for many Russian immigrants during the years it operated, from 1892 until 1954.*

Human beings have always moved from one place to another. Sometimes they have sought territory with more food or better economic conditions. Sometimes they have moved to escape poverty or been forced to flee from invaders who have taken over their territory. When people leave one country or region to settle in another, their movement is called emigration. When people come into a new country or region to settle, it is called immigration. The new arrivals are called immigrants.

People move from their home country to settle in a new land for two underlying reasons. The first reason is that negative conditions in their native land push them to leave. These are called "push factors." People are pushed to emigrate from their native land or region by such things as poverty, religious persecution, or political oppression.

The second reason that people emigrate is that positive conditions in the new country pull them to the new land. These are called "pull factors." People immigrate to new countries seeking opportunities that do not exist in their native country. Push and pull factors often work together. People leave poor conditions in one country seeking better conditions in another.

Sometimes people are forced to flee their homeland because of extreme hardship, war, or oppression. These immigrants to new lands are called refugees. During times of war or famine, large groups of refugees may immigrate to new countries in

search of better conditions. Refugees have been on the move
from the earliest recorded history. Even today, groups of
refugees are forced to move from one country to another.

# Pulled to America

For hundreds of years, people have been pulled to America
seeking freedom and economic opportunity. America has
always been a land of immigrants. The original settlers of
America emigrated from Asia thousands of years ago. These first
Americans were probably following animal herds in search of
better hunting grounds. They migrated to America across a land
bridge that connected the west coast of North America with
Asia. As time passed, they spread throughout North and South
America and established complex societies and cultures.

Beginning in the 1500s, a new group of immigrants came
to America from Europe. The first European immigrants to
America were volunteer sailors and soldiers who were promised
rewards for their labor. Once settlements were established, small
numbers of immigrants from Spain, Portugal, France, Holland,
and England began to arrive. Some were rich, but most were
poor. Most of these emigrants had to pay for the expensive
ocean voyage from Europe to the Western Hemisphere by
promising to work for four to seven years. They were called
indentured servants. These emigrants were pushed out of
Europe by religious persecution, high land prices, and poverty.
They were pulled to America by reports of cheap, fertile land
and by the promise of more religious freedom than they had in
their homelands.

Many immigrants who arrived in America, however, did
not come by choice. Convicts were forcibly transported from
England to work in the American colonies. In addition,

thousands of African men, women, and children were kidnapped in Africa and forced onto slave ships. They were transported to America and forced to work for European masters. While voluntary emigrants had some choice of which territory they would move to, involuntary immigrants had no choice at all. Slaves were forced to immigrate to America from the 1500s until about 1840. For voluntary immigrants, two things influenced where they settled once they arrived in the United States. First, immigrants usually settled where there were jobs. Second, they often settled in the same places as immigrants who had come before them, especially those who were relatives or who had come from the same village or town in their homeland. This is called chain migration. Immigrants felt more comfortable living among people whose language they understood and whom they might have known in the "old country."

Immigrants often came to America with particular skills that they had learned in their native countries. These included occupations such as carpentry, butchering, jewelry making, metal machining, and farming. Immigrants settled in places where they could find jobs using these skills.

In addition to skills, immigrant groups brought their languages, religions, and customs with them to the new land. Each of these many cultures has made unique contributions to American life. Each group has added to the multicultural society that is America today.

# Waves of Immigration

Many immigrant groups came to America in waves. In the early 1800s, economic conditions in Europe were growing harsh. Famine in Ireland led to a massive push of emigration of Irish men and women to the United States. A similar number of

German farmers and urban workers migrated to America. They were attracted by high wages, a growing number of jobs, and low land prices. Starting in 1880, huge numbers of people in southern and eastern Europe, including Italians, Russians, Poles, and Greeks, were facing rising populations and poor economies. To escape these conditions, they chose to immigrate to the United States. In the first 10 years of the 20th century, immigration from Europe was in the millions each year, with a peak of 8 million immigrants in 1910. In the 1930s, thousands of Jewish immigrants fled religious persecution in Nazi Germany and came to America.

# Becoming a Legal Immigrant

There were few limits on the number of immigrants that could come to America until 1924. That year, Congress limited immigration to the United States to only 100,000 per year. In 1965, the number of immigrants allowed into the United States each year was raised from 100,000 to 290,000. In 1986, Congress further relaxed immigration rules, especially for immigrants from Cuba and Haiti. The new law allowed 1.5 million legal immigrants to enter the United States in 1990. Since then, more than half a million people have legally immigrated to the United States each year.

Not everyone who wants to immigrate to the United States is allowed to do so. The number of people from other countries who may immigrate to America is determined by a federal law called the Immigration and Naturalization Act (INA). This law was first passed in 1952. It has been amended (changed) many times since then.

Following the terrorist attacks on the World Trade Center in New York City and the Pentagon in Washington, D.C., in 2001, Congress made significant changes in the INA. One important change was to make the agency that administers laws concerning immigrants and other people entering the United States part of the Department of Homeland Security (DHS). The DHS is responsible for protecting the United States from attacks by terrorists. The new immigration agency is called the Citizenship and Immigration Service (CIS). It replaced the previous agency, which was called the Immigration and Naturalization Service (INS).

When noncitizens enter the United States, they must obtain official permission from the government to stay in the country. This permission is called a visa. Visas are issued by the CIS for a specific time period. In order to remain in the country permanently, an immigrant must obtain a permanent resident visa, also called a green card. This document allows a person to live, work, and study in the United States for an unlimited amount of time.

To qualify for a green card, an immigrant must have a sponsor. In most cases, a sponsor is a member of the immigrant's family who is a U.S. citizen or holds a green card. The government sets an annual limit of 226,000 on the number of family members who may be sponsored for permanent residence. In addition, no more than 25,650 immigrants may come from any one country.

In addition to family members, there are two other main avenues to obtaining a green card. A person may be sponsored by a U.S. employer or may enter the Green Card Lottery. An employer may sponsor a person who has unique work qualifications. The Green Card Lottery randomly selects 50,000 winners each year to receive green cards. Applicants for the lottery may be from any country from which immigration is allowed by U.S. law.

However, a green card does not grant an immigrant U.S. citizenship. Many immigrants have chosen to become citizens of the United States. Legal immigrants who have lived in the United States for at least five years and who meet other requirements may apply to become naturalized citizens. Once these immigrants qualify for citizenship, they become full-fledged citizens and have all the rights, privileges, and obligations of other U.S. citizens.

Even with these newer laws, there are always more people who want to immigrate to the United States than are allowed by law. As a result, some people choose to come to the United States illegally. Illegal immigrants do not have permission from the U.S. government to enter the country. Since 1980, the number of illegal immigrants entering the United States, especially from Central and South America, has increased greatly. These illegal immigrants are pushed by poverty in their homelands and pulled by the hope of a better life in the United States. Illegal immigration cannot be exactly measured, but it is believed that between 1 million and 3 million illegal immigrants enter the United States each year.

This series, Immigration to the United States, describes the history of the immigrant groups that have come to the United States. Some came because of the pull of America and the hope of a better life. Others were pushed out of their homelands. Still others were forced to immigrate as slaves. Whatever the reasons for their arrival, each group has a unique story and has made a unique contribution to the American way of life.

Right: *An elderly Russian Jewish immigrant stands outside a building on Ellis Island in New York Harbor about 1900.*

# Russian Immigration

*Becoming Russian Americans*

Russians are not the largest group of immigrants in American history. They were not one of the earliest groups of immigrants, either. Yet Russian immigrants have made a lasting impact on the United States and the American way of life.

Russian immigrants did not come to the United States in large numbers during its early days, as did some immigrants from other countries. For example, people from England and Germany began arriving in North America in the 1600s. They helped settle the land and build communities. By the time most Russian immigrants arrived in the United States 200 years later, most cities and communities were firmly established. The number of Americans who claim German ancestry today is about 60 million. The number of people who claim Russian ancestry is only about 1 million.

Even so, evidence of Russian culture can be seen and heard throughout the United States. For example, Russian Orthodox churches, which often feature onion-shaped domes, dot the landscape of the United States. Caviar is a Russian delicacy that many people in the United States also enjoy eating. The *Nutcracker Suite* is a well-known ballet often performed during the winter holidays. The music for this ballet was composed by a Russian named Peter Tchaikovsky.

Many other people from Russia have left a lasting impression on the United States. Russian immigrant Igor Sikorsky, for example, came to the United States in 1919. He was a scientist in the new field of aeronautics. In the 1930s, Sikorsky helped design helicopters, which the U.S. military used during World War II. Vladimir Horowitz was a well-known concert pianist who thrilled audiences with his style and talent. Born in 1903 and trained in Russia, he eventually settled in the United States.

People in the United States often find themselves fascinated by people from Russia, mostly because of the traditional differences in each country's political ideas. For the most part, the United States is an open, free society, where people can choose to live and work wherever and however they wish. In Russia, which was at one point in its history part of the former Soviet Union, people did not always have these freedoms. This difference also explains why some people from Russia chose to come to the United States.

# A Land of Czars

Russia is the largest country in the world. Its lands make up more than one-ninth of the world's total landmasses. It spreads across two continents, Europe and Asia. It is almost twice the size of the United States.

# Class System

Russia's government has changed over the course of its history. One of the most significant periods in the story of Russian immigration is that of the rule of the czars.

In 1547, a young prince named Ivan IV was crowned czar of Russia. This was a new title in Russia that demonstrated the power of the new leader. It implied that God had placed Ivan in this position of power. In this new czarist regime, the czar was the absolute ruler of Russia, and Russia's government became an autocracy—a country ruled by a single person or group. The czarist regime would continue in Russia for the next 370 years. Under the czars, every facet of Russian life, including the Russian Orthodox Church and the freedom of both wealthy landowners and poor peasants, was restricted by the government in some way.

In 1613, a sixteen-year-old named Michael Romanov was chosen to be czar. He was the first of the Romanov dynasty, which would rule for the next 300 years, until the end of the czarist regime. Under Michael's rule, and the rule of his son, Alexis, the lives of the peasants became more difficult than they had ever been. The peasants became known as serfs, and their way of life was called serfdom. Their labor was the basis of an economic system called the feudal system.

In some ways, a serf was comparable to a slave. Laws were passed that forbade the peasants to ever leave the lands they farmed. For their entire lives, they were bound by law to farm the same lands, day after day. Their children, and their children's children, were forced to do the same.

# Russian Immigration

Under the czars, many Russian people began to yearn for a better way of life. The serfs, bound to the land by law, desperately wished for their freedom. They wanted to be able to choose what to do with their land and to change their profession if they so desired.

Because of the strict rule of the czarist regime, no large numbers of Russian immigrants came to the United States until the mid-1800s. At that time, the czar gave the serfs a bit of the freedom they wanted. Some serfs chose to remain on a portion of the land they had farmed. Others moved to Russian and European cities, where factories and new industries enabled people to earn a living without working the land. Many Russian serfs left their homeland and made the long journey to the United States.

The story of Russian immigration, however, does not start with a journey across the Atlantic Ocean, nor does it start with the serfs of the mid-1800s. Instead, it starts on the opposite side of the United States—in Alaska. The first immigrants from Russia were not serfs looking for freedom, but Russian fur traders looking for new animals to hunt.

Opposite: *The headquarters of the Russian-American Company in Sitka, Alaska, are pictured in this woodcut from about 1827. Ships were built in Sitka and carried bales of Alaskan furs for sale throughout the world. The furs brought great profits to the first Russian traders in America.*

# Chapter One

# Adventure in the New World

## Early Russian Arrivals

# Russia and
# North America

The first Russians to come to the North American continent came from a different direction than most other explorers of the 1500s and 1600s. On a map, North America and Russia look as if they are half a world apart, with the Atlantic Ocean and the European continent in between. Traveling across the Atlantic Ocean to reach the shores of North America was the way that most European explorers first approached the continent.

North America and Russia, however, are actually very close. The northwestern edge of North America, in Alaska, is just 51 miles (82 km) from the northeastern edge of Russia. It was this northwestern part of North America that the earliest Russians first visited.

*Countries, that along with Russia, composed the Union of Soviet Socialist Republics (USSR).*

# Peter the Great

Peter the Great became the czar of Russia in 1682 at only 10 years of age. As he grew up, he became fascinated by the culture of western Europe, especially that of England and France. Peter began choosing European advisers, who suggested ways to make Russia's military stronger. In response to his advisers' ideas, Peter created a new military that included a navy. Under Peter the Great, Russia's military strength grew, and the country started to become a powerful force on the continents of Europe and Asia.

*Peter I (1672–1725) of Russia, called Peter the Great, introduced Russia to western European civilization and made his country into a recognized European power.*

Peter was also interested in exploring other parts of the world and expanding Russian lands. He ordered the exploration of Siberia, located in the most northern part of Asia, and he also sent explorers eastward across the Asian continent. He believed that the continents of Asia and North America were connected, and he wanted to prove it. In 1725, Peter enlisted a Danish sailor named Vitus Bering to head an expedition east to the area where Peter believed the two continents were connected. Peter also wanted Bering to find out how many European settlements were in North America. In this way, Peter hoped to keep track of his European rivals there. But Peter the Great did not live to see his orders fulfilled. He died that same year.

## First through the Strait

Vitus Bering was not the first person to sail between the closest points of Asia and North America. Peter the Great did not know that, in 1648, a man from Siberia named Semyon Ivanov Dezhnyov had sailed into the Arctic Sea from the Kolyma River off the northeastern coast of Siberia. Dezhnyov took with him 90 men and seven small boats. They traveled south, following the coastline of Asia, and made their way through the strait that separates Asia from North America.

During two expeditions, one in 1728 and one in 1741, Vitus Bering explored the area between Asia and North America. One of the discoveries he made was that the two continents were not connected, as Peter had believed. Instead, they were separated by a strait, or narrow channel of water, that became known as the Bering Strait in honor of the explorer. The sea nearby and an island were also named after Bering.

# The First Russian Immigrants

For some people who lived in Siberia, the land closest to the Bering Strait, the best way to earn a living was to hunt animals for their fur and then sell it. These fur hunters were called *promysloviki*. But by the mid-1700s, many of the animals that once roamed in large numbers across Siberia had been wiped out by the *promysloviki*. Some hunters decided to look for new animals on a different continent—North America.

A Russian named Emelian Basov traveled as far east as Bering Island, which was part of Russia. The furs he brought back prompted other Russian fur hunters to travel eastward. Mikhail Nevodchikov was one of those fur hunters. He reached the westernmost of Alaska's Aleutian Islands on September 25, 1745. He is believed to be the first Russian to set foot on lands that would become part of the United States.

The Russian fur traders began to emigrate to Alaska in earnest. Moving eastward along the chain of Aleutian Islands, the *promysloviki* hunted sea otters, foxes, and northern fur seals. When the hunters had killed nearly all the animals on one island, they moved on to the next. The Native Americans of this area, the Aleut, were horrified by the slaughter but could do little to stop it since their weapons were no match for the Russians' powerful guns.

*This engraving of the harbor of St. Paul, the capital of Russian Alaska, was featured in the book* A Voyage Round the World *in 1814. The book was written by Russian sea captain Urey Lisiansky.*

Eventually, the Russian government, now under the leadership of Empress Catherine II (Catherine the Great), began to restrict the reckless activities of the *promysloviki*. By the 1780s, the Russian fur trade was controlled by six Russian companies. In 1784, Grigory Ivanovich Shelikhov, an owner of one of the companies, landed on Alaska's Kodiak Island. On August 3, Shelikhov, his wife, and 192 men started the first permanent Russian settlement in North America.

## The Push and Pull of the Fur Trade

The Russian fur traders provide a perfect example of the push and pull factors of immigration. The Russian fur traders felt the push to leave Russia because they had exhausted the animal populations there. They felt the pull of a new land where animal populations still thrived in great numbers.

# Russian America

The area in which the Russian fur companies conducted business became known as Russian America. Shelikhov hired a man named Aleksandr Baranov to run his company on Kodiak Island. Baranov's settlement needed supplies, which were hard to get from Russia. So he decided to trade with settlers in the region. These settlers had come from England and the United States. (At that time, the United States consisted of just the original 13 colonies along North America's eastern coast.) Baranov also established a Russian Orthodox church on Kodiak Island in 1794.

In 1799, Shelikhov's company, which had settled Kodiak Island, became the Russian-American Company. The other

Russian fur-trading companies were ordered by the new czar, Paul, to either merge with the Russian-American Company or disband. Now that there was just one Russian fur-trading company, Aleksandr Baranov was able to expand the territories of Russian America. In 1804, he established the settlement of Novo-Arkhangel'sk on Alaska's mainland. Today this settlement is the town of Sitka. In 1808, Sitka became the capital of Russian America.

# From Alaska to California

Life in Alaska for the Russian settlers was not easy. The climate was cold and harsh, and food was often scarce. The winter of 1805–1806 was particularly difficult. Supply ships from Russia were unable to reach Alaska because of bad weather. Nikolay Petrovich Rezanov, an official with the Russian-American Company, newly arrived in Sitka, described the situation as "disastrous."

Rezanov decided that the best way to get supplies for the Russians in Alaska was to venture southward along the west coast of North America to trade with Spanish settlers in California. (In the early 1800s, California was owned by Spain.) Although the Russian government did not want to trade with the Spanish, Rezanov felt he had no choice. He sailed into San Francisco Bay and met with the Spanish leader there in 1806. This meeting paved the way for the Russians to begin moving south.

Starting in 1808, Aleksandr Baranov, the leader of the Russian-American Company, sent his assistant, Ivan Alexandrovich Kuskov, on several expeditions into California. Just north of San Francisco, Kuskov chose a site for a new Russian settlement in Bodega Bay. Established in 1811, it became known as Fort Ross.

## The United States

Alaska and the East Coast of North America are separated by several thousand miles. In the 1770s, the United States was fighting for independence from England in the Revolutionary War and had no interest in the Russian settlement on the other side of the continent. As the Russian settlements expanded in the 1780s and 1790s, the United States was slowly growing into a nation:

• In 1784, when Russian settlers arrived on Kodiak Island, the United States was still working to define its government. The U.S. Constitution was created during the summer of 1787.

George Washington would not be elected the country's first president until 1789.

• In 1794, when the first Russian Orthodox church was established on Kodiak Island, George Washington was serving his second term as president.

• In 1808, when Sitka was named the capital of Russian America, Thomas Jefferson was serving his second term as the third president of the United States. With the Louisiana Purchase of 1803, the United States had doubled in size. Now the United States was spreading westward.

# Life at Fort Ross

Fort Ross was the first Russian settlement in California. Its primary function was to make money for the Russian-American Company. About 100 Russian settlers—laborers, fishermen, and hunters, who hunted sea otters for their fur—lived at Fort Ross. Most of them worked for the company.

Life at Fort Ross was much easier than it had been in Alaska. The weather was warmer, which made it easier to grow enough food. Over the next 30 years, the settlement expanded. It had a windmill, cattle yard, farm buildings, bathhouses, and a cemetery. Along the river (eventually named the Russian River) that fed into Bodega Bay, the settlers built a tannery (a place to make leather), a forge (a place to make tools from iron and other metals), a storage shed, and a boathouse. They also built a Russian Orthodox church, which still stands today.

The Native Americans of the area of California around Fort Ross were the Kashaya. Fort Ross was built on Kashaya land. The Kashaya exchanged the land for Russian tools and trinkets. In 1817, the Russians and the Kashaya signed a deed giving the land to the Russians. The deed is believed to be the only document ever signed by Europeans and Native Americans of California. The Russians gave the chief of the Kashaya, Chu-gu-an, a medal inscribed with the words "Allies of Russia." The Kashaya and the Russians lived together peacefully for many years.

The Russian influence in the area was vast. Because of the close relationship between the Russians and the Native Americans,

*The Russian settlement of Bodega (Fort Ross) on the coast of New Albion (California) is shown in this lithograph from 1833.*

many Russian words crept into Native American languages. Many Russian men married Native American women and started families. Although it was still a remote settlement, for many years Fort Ross was a comfortable place to live.

## Russian Orthodox Church

The Russian Orthodox Church was the only church recognized by the Russian government, and everyone in Russia had to belong to it. The Russian Orthodox religion is a Christian faith that follows the teachings in the Bible. The practices of the Russian Orthodox Church are very formal and ceremonial. Church services may last for several hours. Incense burns in round metal containers, which the priests swing on chains to spread the incense smoke, and the priests chant the service rather than speak it. Building Russian Orthodox churches in remote settlements was one way for the Russians in Alaska to stay connected to their homeland.

By the 1830s, the sea otter population began to dwindle because of overhunting. The sea otter had been the Russian-American Company's main export. The Russians finally gave up and on January 1, 1842, the last Russian ship departed Bodega Bay. In 1867, Russia sold all of its lands in Alaska to the United States. Russia's presence in North America had ended.

Opposite: *When Russian and other immigrants arrived in the United States, they were often forced to receive vaccinations against diseases such as smallpox. Many immigrants thought the inoculations would make them sick so they resisted.*

# Chapter Two

# Poverty and Passage

## The Flight to America

*Russian settlers in North America built farming and trading villages
such as this one, shown in a 19th-century illustration.*

# Finding Freedom

The Russian settlers in Alaska and California in the early
19th century had something that most people in Russia
did not have—freedom. Although the Russian settlers worked for
the Russian-American Company, they were not bound by the
very strict laws of the Russian government. Instead, they had the
freedom to move around and to investigate and learn about
western North America. Back home in Russia, however, most

Russians were oppressed by the government. This oppression would lead to several revolutions, which in turn would lead thousands of people to emigrate from Russia.

In the 1800s, Russia was a land of discontent. The czars continued to rule over the Russian empire, and they gave important jobs in the government and the military to rich landowning nobles. Only 5 or 10 percent of the Russian population belonged to this elite group.

The other 90 percent of the Russian population, the serfs, were far less fortunate. The lives of the serfs continued to worsen. The nobles considered the serfs as property. For instance, if the nobles sold their land, the serfs who worked the land were sold along with it. Sometimes the nobles traded their serfs for items they wanted. And because the serfs were considered no more than property, many were cruelly mistreated by the landowners.

The Russian czars also wanted to make Russia completely Russian. As the Russian empire grew, it took over countries with

> # It's a Fact!
>
> **Leo Tolstoy (1828–1910) is one of Russia's most well-known authors. His novel *War and Peace* reflects Russian life during the historic time period of the Napoleonic Wars, between 1799 and 1815, when Russia fought against several European countries.**

various ethnic groups, such as the Poles, Latvians, Balts, and Lithuanians. These people were ordered to speak Russian and adopt Russian traditions.

Another group that was persecuted was the Jews who lived in the Russian empire. When Russia conquered Poland in 1831, Poland had a Jewish population of about a million people. Because the Jewish people did not practice the official Russian Orthodox religion of Russia, the Russian government saw the Jews as a threat. People in Poland who were not Jewish were able to keep most of the rights they had before Russia took over. The Jews, however, could keep their rights only if they remained in the same place as before the Russians arrived. This meant that Jews did not have the freedom to move about if they wanted to. In addition, Jews were not allowed to own land in the countryside, so they had no choice but to live in towns and cities.

As time passed, the area in which these now Russian Jews lived became known as the Pale of Settlement, or the pale. Jews were not permitted to move beyond the boundaries of the pale or to conduct business outside the pale. As a result, Jewish crafts-people who had depended on trade throughout their region found themselves without work. In addition, the Russian govern-ment forced Jewish men to serve for 25 years in the Russian army. Jewish boys were forced to serve from the ages of 12 to 18 in special army regiments.

## Inside the Pale

At first, life inside the pale was not much different than life for the Jews had been before Russia took over Poland. Each shtetl, or Jewish village, within the pale had a synagogue—a Jewish house of worship—and a shopping area. Most people in the shtetl worked at this marketplace. As the years passed, however, the conditions within the pale worsened. As families grew, space and resources became scarce. Soon, people within the pale were living in poverty.

Ultimately, the Russian government wanted the "Russification" of everyone who lived within the empire. People who had different traditions, backgrounds, or religions were persecuted and forced to conform. The serfs in particular became increasingly unhappy with their treatment at the hands of their landlords. People started demanding a change.

# Freedom!

Under the feudal system, the peasants were not able to move freely about Russia, and they certainly were not allowed to emigrate from Russia to Europe or the United States. Like African-American slaves in the United States during this time, Russian serfs met with harsh consequences if they tried to escape from the farms on which they worked. In that way, the serfs were also similar to Russian Jews, who had to remain within the Pale of Settlement.

In 1854, Russia was engaged in war against France and Britain. Many serfs were forced into military duty, and they were promised that after the war they would be freed. When the war ended, the Russian government broke this promise. The serfs were furious.

Alexander II became the czar of Russia in 1855. Alexander was very much aware of the serfs' unhappiness. He feared that Russia would have a major revolution if the serfs were not appeased. So in 1861, Alexander put forth many reforms to improve the lives of the serfs. In the process, more than 20 million serfs, about half of the serf population, were granted their freedom. All the serfs were eventually granted their freedom as the practice of serfdom was slowly brought to an end.

## It's a Fact!

The serfs of Russia were granted their freedom before the slaves in the United States. In the United States, slaves would not have their freedom until 1865, four years after Alexander II had freed many of the serfs.

Many serfs thought that upon getting their freedom, they would be given the lands that their families had farmed for generations. In most cases, however, the serfs retained only very small plots of land. The plots were too small to sustain an entire family. As families grew and plots were divided among siblings, families had even less land to farm.

Even so, the serfs' lives under Alexander II had improved overall, as did the lives of Jewish people. In 1859, Alexander changed the laws so that Jews could once again move outside the pale. Many Jews left their small shtetls and settled in large cities, such as St. Petersburg, Moscow, and Odessa. In addition, Jewish boys were no longer forced to serve in the army. Alexander also made it possible for Jewish children to attend Russian schools.

Alexander II was truly trying to make life better for all Russians. He encouraged the government to be less restrictive in its policies. He established new schools and hospitals. He even established a court system that allowed trial by jury.

*This engraving shows Czar Alexander II in his formal military uniform. Alexander ruled Russia from 1855 to 1881.*

*Russian Jews are shown congregating in the streets of Odessa, Russia,
around 1800. They are wearing traditional clothing. Many Russian
Jews immigrated to U.S. cities seeking jobs in American factories.*

# Pulled toward New Shores

For the first time in their lives, the Russian serfs had choices
about where they could live. They could stay on their small
plots of land or move to another part of Russia. They could try
to make a living in a city rather than in the countryside. They
could even leave Russia and venture to a new land, where they
could live freely and enjoy more opportunities than the lower
classes had in Russia. For many poor Russians, this new land was
the United States.

During the mid-1800s, the Industrial Revolution had taken
hold in the United States and in Europe. This wave of industri-
alism took a bit longer to reach Russia, but eventually it did so

in the latter half of the 1800s. In western Russia, factories now provided work for many farmers who no longer had land.

In the United States also, factories provided work for the many immigrants flowing into the country. Countless stories about the riches to be earned in the United States, if one was willing to work hard, drifted back to Russia. For many serfs, who had worked hard all their lives, the attraction of the United States was too great to ignore. First, however, they had to make a very long journey.

# Russian-American Civil War Officer

One Russian immigrant distinguished himself so dramatically in the Civil War that he became a general in the U.S. Army. Formerly a colonel in the Russian army, Ivan Turchaninov arrived in the United States in 1856 with his wife, Nadezhda. Because his name was difficult for Americans to pronounce, Turchaninov changed his name to Turchin. Together, he and his wife enjoyed the opportunities they found in America. Turchin became an engineer for a railroad company, and Nadezhda practiced medicine. When the Civil War erupted in the United States in 1861, Turchin joined the Union, or Northern, army. He became a colonel, and Nadezhda worked as a nurse. Although Turchin was accused of encouraging his troops to treat civilians cruelly during an attack in Georgia, President Abraham Lincoln did not agree. Lincoln promoted Turchin to the rank of brigadier general. In 1856 Turchin wrote:

*I thank America for one thing: it helped me get rid of my aristocratic prejudices and reduced me to the ranks of all mortals. I have been reborn: I fear no work; no sphere of business scares me away and no social position will put me down; it makes no difference whether I plow and cart manure or sit in a richly decorated room and discuss astronomy with great scholars of the New World. I want to earn the right to call myself a citizen of the United States of North America.*

# Traveling to America

The decision to leave their homeland and emigrate to America was not easy for the Russian peasants. Not only were they leaving behind everything and everyone they had known, but the trip itself was difficult and costly.

Even though travel through Russia was not as restrictive as it once had been, people still needed permission if they wanted to leave. Special documents were needed and were often not granted. Some people sneaked out of the country or obtained false papers. Some people saved extra money so they could bribe Russian officials to let them leave or officials at the borders of other countries to let them enter.

In the 1800s, airplanes and cars had yet to be invented. The quickest way to leave Russia was by train. The trains were often very crowded and uncomfortable. The trip was long and tiring, with no place to sleep and very little space to even sit down. These trains brought the emigrants to European port cities, such as Hamburg, Germany, where the emigrants could board steamships going to the United States.

The port cities were often a shock to the emigrants. For many, it was their first time away from rural farmlands, and the crowds, the city buildings, and the confusing foreign languages were likely to be overwhelming.

Arriving at the port city, even with the proper documents and enough money to buy a ticket, did not guarantee that a person would be able to sail for the United States right away. Hopeful emigrants often had to wait for a ship to arrive, discharge its cargo, and prepare to sail again before they could embark. This wait could take weeks, even months. Emigrants found themselves living in temporary villages, set up primarily to house the people waiting to go to America.

After traveling across Europe on a train and waiting in a port city, the emigrants had another test to pass—the approval of the shipping officials. To prevent diseases from breaking out on board the ship, passengers were examined to make sure they were in good health. Sometimes their hair was cut off to protect against lice. Clothes and luggage might also be thoroughly cleaned before the emigrants were allowed on board. The officials knew that if the emigrants were turned away by American officials, the shipping company would have to pay for their return ticket back to Europe. The officials therefore tried to ensure that everyone bound for the United States would be given entry into the country.

Finally the ship began its slow journey across the Atlantic Ocean. Most Russian emigrants booked passage in the steerage section of the ship, which was the cheapest. This section was at the bottom of the ship, and it could hold up to a thousand people. Passengers in steerage were not allowed to venture to the topmost levels of the ship. They were granted some time outdoors on their own decks, which alleviated the crowded, dirty conditions of steerage.

The steerage section of a typical immigrant steamship was not a pleasant place. It had no windows and no fresh air. People were packed into small rooms. Meals were eaten at long tables. Luggage was piled everywhere. The smell of human bodies and waste and spoiled food, along with the rolling of the ship, was enough to make many people sick.

Yet despite these hardships, emigrants continued to make the journey, trading their past lives in Russia for their dreams of a better future in America. The challenge of adapting to life in America was yet to come. ✷

Opposite: *Polish and Russian passengers are crowded on the deck in the steerage section of a ship heading to America in the early 1900s.*

*Chapter Three*

# A New Life in
America

*1880–1920*

# The Great Wave

Between 1880 and 1930, the United States saw its biggest influx of immigrants, and the third-largest group to immigrate–some 3.3 million people–came from the Russian empire. (The largest group, 4.6 million, came from Italy, followed by 4 million from the Austro-Hungarian Empire.) Some were former serfs looking for a better way of life. Some were Russian Jews trying to escape persecution. Others were members of the privileged class in Russia. Once they landed in the United States, however, these Russians all became Americans.

# Port of Entry

Most immigrants arriving in the United States came through the port city of New York. Before 1892, immigrants were processed in lower Manhattan at a place called Castle Garden. But the facilities at Castle Garden were not adequate to handle the thousands of people now arriving in the United States every day. So in 1892, the port of entry for immigrants changed from Castle Garden to a new immigration center, Ellis Island.

Ellis Island welcomed a diverse mixture of people from all over the world, all hoping to gain entry to the United States so they could start a new life. First, though, they had to endure the rigorous steps of immigration processing.

## It's a Fact!

Ellis Island is named after Samuel Ellis. He bought the island in the 1700s and named it after himself. Before Ellis bought it, the island was called Gibbet Island because a pirate had been hanged there in 1765. (A gibbet is a gallows, a high, upright frame that was used to hang criminals.)

*This inspection card from the Ellis Island collection shows that the Russian immigrant in berth 128 of a passenger ship from the Russian-Asiatic Steamship Company passed inspection after a 16-day stay.*

Once at Ellis Island and off the ships that had carried them across the ocean, the immigrants entered Registry Hall. The hall was a giant room packed with people. Here, the immigrants were inspected by health officials. The officials wanted to make sure that no immigrants brought dangerous diseases into the country. Part of the health inspection was an eye examination. The eyes could sometimes reveal signs of illness. Even though most immigrants had been checked by health officials in the country where they had boarded their ships, U.S. officials took this extra precaution. If the U.S. health officials suspected that someone was ill, that person was quarantined, or kept in a separate room for several days. After that time, the health officials determined if the person was healthy enough to enter the country.

Immigrants who passed the health and eye inspections moved on to the next stage of immigration processing—a personal interview. The immigrants had to answer questions about their skills, how they planned to make a living in the United States, if they had any family in the United States, and why they wanted to come to America. The interviewers wanted to make sure that none of the immigrants would be dangerous to their adopted country or become dependent on others.

At long last, after a perilous journey across Europe, several weeks at sea, and a grueling immigration process at Ellis Island, immigrants were given a document stating that they had the legal right to be in the United States. Finally, they were able to start their new lives in America.

# Tenement Life

Immigrants arriving from Russia and other countries did not know what to expect in New York. They had heard stories about "streets paved in gold." But as they stepped off the boat that took them from Ellis Island to Manhattan, they learned that the streets were covered not in gold, but in stone, just like the streets in Russia. People surged through the city, speaking a variety of exotic-sounding languages. Horses clopped past, vendors called from street corners, and buildings stood several stories high. For most newcomers, the scene was both frightening and exciting.

If the immigrants were fortunate, they knew someone in New York. If the immigrants were complete strangers to the city, they searched for a neighborhood where they felt most comfortable. This was likely to be a neighborhood with other immigrants who had come from Russia. For many Russian immigrants in the late 1800s and early 1900s, that neighborhood was the Lower East Side of Manhattan.

As the officials at the old Castle Garden immigration center had realized, New York was not prepared to handle the huge influx of immigrants from around the world in the late 1800s. Before 1840, about 300,000 people lived in New York City. During the 1840s, the population nearly doubled to more than 500,000. In the 1850s, the population rose to more than 800,000. Yet the biggest wave of immigration would not reach New York for several more decades.

The increase in population forced most people in New York, particularly poor immigrants, to live in very small, cramped apartments in buildings called tenements. Several families might live in one tenement apartment. The apartment might have a toilet and a bathtub, but many did not. Toilets and bathtubs were often shared by others on the same floor of the tenement building. Sometimes toilets were located outside.

## The Council's Report

People concerned with the cramped living conditions in New York tenements formed a committee called the Council of Hygiene and Public Health. This group wanted to prevent the spread of yellow fever and cholera—two deadly diseases. The council's survey discovered that nearly half a million people in New York City in 1864 lived in overcrowded tenements—about half the city's population. The council's survey concluded:

*It is only because the rate of packing is somewhat diminished by intervening warehouses, factories, private dwellings, and other classes of buildings that the entire tenement-house population is not devastated by the domestic pestilences [such as rats] and infectious epidemics [disease] that arise from overcrowding and uncleanness. . . . Such concentration and packing of a population has probably never been equaled in any city as may be found in particular localities in New York.*

*This drawing shows what life was like on the busy streets of a Russian Jewish neighborhood in New York City in the 1890s.*

# Earning a Living

M any Russians who came to the United States during the late 1800s and early 1900s had been farmers. But as poor immigrants, they had no money to purchase land to farm in the United States. Most of the immigrants stayed in the city to earn a living, even though they had few skills.

To make money, many Russian immigrants took jobs in city factories, which usually required no special skills. Some factories required that their laborers work 12 hours a day, seven days a week. Breaks for lunch or to use the bathroom were extremely limited and often monitored. At that time, very few laws existed to protect workers from the factory owners' harsh demands. Even children went to work in factories to contribute to the family's earnings.

Many immigrant women found employment in New York's garment (clothing manufacturing) district. According to historians' estimates, about 500 blouse factories operated in New York in the early 1900s. They employed about 40,000 workers, most of whom were Russian Jewish immigrants. Women could also do sewing at home. Since workers were often paid according to the amount of clothing they stitched, not the amount of time they worked, being able to work at home meant that the women could work longer hours than on a factory shift, thus earning more money.

Some Russian immigrants moved westward into Pennsylvania and became coal miners, digging underground for coal, which was used as fuel to heat homes and other buildings. Other immigrants took jobs in steel mills, processing raw materials into metals that could be used in construction and made into many products, such as tools and machine parts.

None of these jobs were creative or fulfilling. Some were dangerous. The hours were long, the work was tiring and dirty, the working conditions were unhealthy, and the pay was low. But these jobs did not require much training, education, or knowledge of the English language, so they were the only kinds of work that most immigrants could find.

Even though life for Russian immigrants was often harsh, many flourished in their new homeland. They had been used to living in crowded conditions in Russia, so tenements overflowing with people did not bother them. For some, indoor plumbing was a new luxury. But perhaps the biggest change of all was the increase in wages. Although the working day was long and tedious, Russian immigrants were able to earn and save more money than they could in Russia. Many were able to start businesses of their own. Seamstresses sewed clothes at home. Peddlers (people who travel from place to place in order to sell goods) sold clothing and food from carts that they rolled down the streets and sidewalks.

## The American St. Petersburg

Pyotr Alexeyevitch Dementev was born in Russia in 1850, about 200 miles (320 km) southeast of St. Petersburg. Dementev served as a captain in the Imperial Guard of Czar Alexander II. After the czar was assassinated in 1881, Dementev decided to emigrate to the United States. He arrived in America in 1881, settled in Florida, and changed his name to Peter Demens. A year after arriving in the United States, Demens sent for his wife and four children, who had remained behind in Russia. Demens worked to establish a railroad line in Florida, and he helped found the town of St. Petersburg on Florida's west coast, which he named after the Russian city near his birthplace.

# Russian Communities

Most Russians in New York City lived in neighborhoods with other Russians, where the language, foods, and traditions of their homeland were all around them. Many Russian Jews felt safe for the first time in New York, where they were no longer persecuted for their religious beliefs. In Pennsylvania, Russians who worked in the steel mills and coal mines lived in boardinghouses—homes that rented rooms, usually to single people. Gradually, as political conditions in Russia continued to push immigrants to the United States, communities of Russian immigrants were established.

# Back Home in Russia

Upon the assassination of Czar Alexander II in 1881, Alexander III became czar. But unlike his predecessor, who had tried to reform the Russian government, Alexander III wanted the Russian government to once again become a strict, all-powerful regime.

Under new laws imposed by Alexander III, Jews were once again restricted in their movements. The size of the pale settlements was reduced by 10 percent, which meant that many Jews had to leave their homes because their homes were no longer part of the pale. Buying goods, selling property, and working outside the pale was once again limited.

The most devastating acts against Russian Jews during this time were the pogroms. A pogrom was a raid on a Jewish settlement, usually conducted by Russian citizens and a group called the Cossacks. The first pogrom occurred in 1881 in a small

*This illustration from the 1880s shows Jews being attacked by a mob while police look on in Kiev, Russia.*

town called Yelizavetgrad. During a pogrom, Jewish property was damaged or destroyed, people were beaten and killed, and families were left homeless. Incited by a fear of the Jewish religion and culture, Russian civilians instigated countless pogroms throughout eastern Russia, killing thousands of Jews in the process.

Alexander III's tyrannical reign did not stop with the oppression of the Jews. He believed that all wealth should be owned and controlled by the government. To meet this end, he stripped many wealthy landowners of their lands and possessions. Consequently, many aristocratic families chose to leave Russia, along with the serfs and the Jews.

## Under the Czar

David Von Drehle, a reporter for the *Washington Post*, wrote a book about a historic fire in one of New York City's garment factories. The book describes a Russian Jewish family and the plight of all eastern Europeans during the czarist regime:

*In 1903, [Clara] Lemlich and her family joined the flood of roughly two million Eastern European Jewish immigrants that entered the United States between 1881 and the end of World War I [1918]. This was one of the largest, and most influential, migrations in history—roughly a third of the Jewish population in the East left their homes for a new life, and most of them found it in America. What was distinctive about the emigration was that an entire culture pulled up stakes and moved. It was not just the poor, or the young and foot-loose, or the politically vanquished that left. Faced with ever more crushing oppression and escalating anti-Jewish violence, the professional classes, stripped of their positions, had reason to leave. So did parents eager to save their sons from mandatory service in the czar's army; so did the idealists frustrated by backsliding conditions, as did the* luftmenschen, *the unskilled poor who had no clear way of supporting themselves in a harsh land.*

Cossacks were Russian people who lived primarily in Siberia. When the Russian empire expanded its territory into Siberia, it absorbed the Cossacks into Russia. As a result, Cossack men were forced into military service. The Cossacks became excellent fighters, remaining their own, unique fighting group, apart from the rest of the Russian army. The Russian government often used the fierce Cossack fighters for special missions, such as the pogroms that destroyed Jewish settlements and killed Jewish people.

# The End of the Czars

Alexander III died in 1894, and his son Nicholas became Czar Nicholas II. Russia would continue to be a land of unrest under his reign. The more the people protested against the oppression of the czar and the Russian government, the more Nicholas II tightened his control. Violence was quick to erupt, and Nicholas began arresting people he believed had committed political crimes.

Russians starting forming political groups that favored an alternative form of government. The groups, or councils, were called soviets. The soviets showed people in cities throughout Russia how to hold demonstrations against the Russian government. The soviets also supplied their supporters with weapons.

In 1914, Russia faced a new threat—World War I. When Archduke Ferdinand, the heir to the throne of the Austrian empire, was assassinated, the Austrians blamed the country of Serbia. Russia came to Serbia's defense, and Germany took Austria's side. France and England fought on the side of the Russians and Serbs. At first, the people of Russia supported the czar in the war. But after several major battles, it became obvious that the Russian government under the czar was not prepared for war. After three years, between 6 and 8 million Russian soldiers were dead, wounded, or missing. Nearly 4 million soldiers were killed during the first year of the war alone.

Faced with the failure of the Russian military, Nicholas decided in 1915 that his job should be leading the troops, not leading the country. He left Russia to fight in the war in Europe. In the meantime, peasants from around the country fled to the cities to escape the war. Petrograd (formerly St. Petersburg) was overrun with refugees, and food was soon in short supply. Hungry, tired of the war, and angry with the czarist government, people in Petrograd began to revolt in February 1917. The Petrograd guard (similar to a police force) joined the peasants in the revolution. The Russian government was powerless to stop it. On March 15, 1917, Nicholas II stepped down as the czar of Russia.

The beginning of the Russian Revolution in 1917 and the end of World War I in 1918 led to radical changes in Russia, starting with the end of the czarist regime. These changes affected Russian immigration, which would decline over the next decades. Meanwhile, Russian Americans slowly adjusted to their new lives in America.

Opposite: *A group of Russian exiles is shown on the deck of the U.S. Army transport ship* Merritt *in 1923. These immigrants landed in San Francisco, California, after escaping from Communist Russia.*

# Chapter Four

# Russian
# Communities

## The Lives of the Immigrants

# Prejudices in a New Land

When Russian immigrants first began arriving in the United States in large numbers at the end of the 19th century, they faced prejudice from many Americans. Before the 1880s, Russian emigration had been extremely limited. Many Americans had never met anyone from Russia. The Russians' poverty and inability to speak English gave some Americans the impression that the Russian immigrants were inferior as people. Instead of welcoming these foreigners, many Americans chose to treat them harshly or to simply ignore them.

These prejudices compelled many Russian immigrants to live in communities where they felt most comfortable—communities in which mostly Russian people lived. This practice was not unusual. Immigrants from other countries also tended to live in neighborhoods with people from their own homeland. In New York City, for example, Italian immigrants formed a neighborhood that is today still called "Little Italy." In many cities across America, including New York and San Francisco, immigrants from China also lived in close-knit neighborhoods called "Chinatowns."

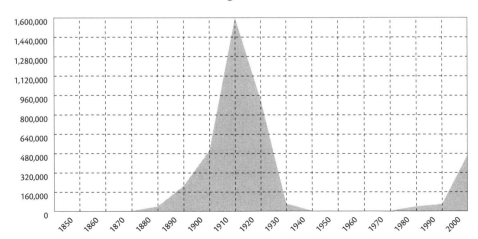

**Russian Immigration to America**

Because of the hostility that Russian immigrants often felt from other Americans, many chose to stay within their communities, associating only with other Russians. In these communities, they continued to speak the Russian language and practice Russian traditions. They established Russian Orthodox churches so they could continue to worship as they had in Russia.

Not all Russian immigrants chose to stay in New York. Because some had been farmers in Russia, they moved outside the city into rural parts of New Jersey and New York State. Many others chose to settle on the West Coast, lured by the growth of the western states. Between 1880 and 1917, historians estimate that about 50,000 Russian immigrants settled in California, Oregon, Washington State, and British Columbia in Canada.

While many Russian immigrants who came to the United States were single people, some families also made the journey. Life was very difficult for Russian families in America. The father, considered the head of the household, usually left early in the morning, worked a grueling day in a factory, then returned home late in the evening. The mother remained home to care for the children and the home (usually an apartment in a tenement building). Often she would also earn money at home by sewing or washing other people's clothes.

Russian children were often more adaptable to life in America than their parents. They went to school with English-speaking American children. As the Russian children learned English, they began to dress, speak, and act as American children did.

When the children in the family had learned to speak English, they often served as translators for their parents. In this way, many older Russian immigrants were able to communicate with people outside their Russian communities. At the same time, they had no urgent need to learn English because their children could now speak for them. This tended to isolate the older Russians from American life even more.

Russian neighborhoods and communities in America were very important to Russian immigrants. Many communities had Russian clubs, where immigrants could enjoy Russian traditions and culture while making friends with other Russians. Although they might live within the same communities, immigrants had little time to socialize between working and raising families. Russian clubs encouraged them to meet and make friends in their new country.

## Mutual Aid Societies

Today, the U.S. government has programs that help people who do not have a lot of money. But before the 1930s, no such programs existed. Many immigrant groups formed organizations to help others. These groups were called mutual aid societies. Russian Americans formed such groups as Mutual Aid for Russian Workers and the Ukranian National Home. People in these organizations helped immigrants adapt to their new country by helping them find housing and jobs. These groups also provided something else that was very important to the immigrants—people who spoke their language.

# Russian Jews in America

Like other Russians, the Russian Jews who emigrated to America faced similar prejudices. Russian Jews often settled in communities in which other Jews lived, including Jewish people from other countries, such as Germany and Poland. In addition to the Jewish communities in major cities such as New York, smaller Jewish communities such as those in Buffalo, New York, and Clarksburg, West Virginia, also became popular with

Russian Jews. Some Russian Jews joined Russian clubs with Russian Christians, but were generally more comfortable remaining among other Russian Jews.

Russian Jews who were financially able often chose to start their own businesses. Beginning as peddlers, they sold food and household items. Eventually, many peddlers were able to establish their own shops. These shops, usually set up in their own neighborhoods, often specialized in Russian or kosher foods. (*Kosher* refers to a special way of preparing food that Jewish people eat.) Sometimes customers from outside the community might buy something from these shops, but most of the shops' customers were people from the surrounding neighborhood.

# Speaking Russian

Some Russian words have become part of the English language:

**cosmonaut:** a Russian astronaut

**mammoth:** very large; derived from the Russian word *mammot,* or mole; name given to a large elephant-like prehistoric animal first found in Siberia in 1806

**samovar:** an urn used to boil water, especially for tea

**steppe:** dry, treeless grassland, usually in Asia; derived from the Russian word *step*

**troika:** a group of three, especially in reference to a government

**tundra:** a treeless area, usually in very cold climates, like the Arctic

**vodka:** an alcoholic beverage that is clear, like water; in Russian, *vodka* means "water"

# One Child's Story

F rederick Trutkoff was born in January 1932 in the Bronx, a
section of New York City. His father owned the building in
which the family lived. It housed mostly Russian people. Both of
Frederick's parents had immigrated to the United States from
Russia in the 1920s, but the details of their immigration were not
clear to him. "[I] didn't ask them, and they didn't volunteer infor-
mation," Trutkoff recalls. "They never wanted to talk about it."

Frederick and his parents lived in a Russian neighborhood in
New York, and they chose to speak Russian at home. "When I was
young, everyone around me spoke Russian," he recalls. "I didn't
realize that I wasn't speaking the same language as other kids [in
the Bronx] until I went to
school. I couldn't understand
the teacher or the other
students! I had to learn how
to speak English."

Trutkoff also remembers
spending summers at Rova
Farms, a Russian cultural
center and meeting place in
Ocean County, New Jersey.
Rova Farms was established
by Russian Americans in the
1920s. Some Russian
immigrants who had been
farmers in Russia and settled
in New York had never
completely adapted to life in
the big city. As soon as they
had saved enough money,

*Russian immigrant Jessie Malik
is shown sorting eggs from
chickens she raised in the
Russian immigrant community
in Lakewood, New Jersey, in 1937.*

many chose to settle in more rural areas, such as those available in the neighboring state of New Jersey. Rova Farms became a cultural meeting place for Russian Americans, and during the summer, it served as a camp for Russian-American children.

"We used to go swimming in the lake," Trutkoff says. "We also attended Russian Orthodox ceremonies at Saint Vladimir's church." The church was also on the grounds of Rova Farms.

*Russian immigrant and ragtime music composer Irving Berlin is shown in his New York office in this photograph from 1911.*

## Irving Berlin

***

One of the most patriotic songs about the United States, "God Bless America," was actually written by a Russian immigrant named Irving Berlin. His real name was Isidore Baline, and he was born in Russia in the late 1880s. He immigrated to the United States with his family in 1893. Berlin's first song was published in 1907, and eventually he became one of the greatest composers in American music history. In 1921, he helped finance the construction of the Music Box Theater in New York City. He also wrote numerous Broadway shows, including *Annie Get Your Gun* (1946), and his songs appeared in such movies as *Top Hat* (1935) and *Easter Parade* (1948). One of Berlin's most popular songs is "White Christmas."

For many Russian immigrants, adapting to life in the United States was a difficult process. Russian communities offered support and familiarity, but they also often kept Russians from meeting other Americans. Along with the prejudices faced by many immigrant groups, this slowed the acceptance of Russian immigrants in the United States. Even so, life for Russian Americans would eventually improve as life for most of their fellow Russians back home would continue to decline.

# From Russia to the USSR

When Czar Nicholas II stepped down from power on March 15, 1917, the czarist regime in Russia came to an end. This date also marks the beginning of the Russian Revolution and the rise of the Bolsheviks, or Communist Party. The Communists were led by a man named Vladimir Ilich Ulyanov, who became known as V. I. Lenin. When Lenin's Communist government took over the country, Russia was renamed the Union of Soviet Socialist Republics (USSR).

The Russian Revolution lasted until 1921. When it ended, the Communist government was firmly in power in the country formerly known as Russia. The new government took control of all Russian lands, including those owned by the Russian Orthodox Church, the nobles, and the peasants. Businesses were no longer owned by individuals, but by the government. In fact, the government controlled everything, even the distribution of food.

With so much control over land, business, and consumer products, the Communist government hoped to create a society in which everyone was equal. The Communists wanted a society where there were no privileged people, such as royal families and nobles, ruling over peasants and workers. For many Russian peasants, such radical change signaled a new and better way of life.

*Vladimir Ilich Ulyanov, who became known as V. I. Lenin, sits at a table during a meeting of the Bolshevik Party in 1918.*

# Sympathizers to Analyzers

P eople in the United States watched what was happening in Russia with interest. At first, many supported the Russian Revolution. The United States itself had fought against a tyrannical monarchy in the American Revolution. People in the United States also believed that everyone should have an equal chance to work, vote, and participate in the government.

Soon, however, many people in the United States began to analyze and find fault with the new form of government. The ideals of the Communist system contrasted sharply with the ideals of the capitalist system of the United States. In the USSR, for example, the Communist government owned and controlled everything, including land, businesses, and the production of items such as food. Individual people were not allowed to own property or produce items for individual profit; people were supposed to work together for the common good. In the United States, individuals were encouraged to own land and businesses. People were free to pursue their own interests.

The new conditions in Russia created a new era of immigration to the United States. Unlike the Russian immigrants who had come before, this new wave of Russian immigrants would have a strong voice in how they were treated in their new homeland. In 1924, a ruthless dictator named Joseph Stalin took over the Soviet government. As his version of communism, known as Stalinism, became firmly entrenched in the Soviet Union, many Americans began to question the loyalty of their Russian-American neighbors.

# It's a Fact!

The Russian language does not use the same alphabet as the English language. The Russian language uses the Cyrillic alphabet, and its letters or symbols look very different from the ABCs that American children learn. When they learn English, Russian immigrants must learn not only new words but also an entirely new alphabet.

Opposite: *Boston police are shown in 1919 with a haul of "subversive" literature, which they confiscated during the post-World War I Red Scare. During this time, the police raided many Russian immigrant groups because they suspected them of being communist organizations that were plotting against the U.S. government.*

# Chapter Five

# Worlds Collide

## *1920—1945*

# The New Russian Immigrants

The Russian Revolution of 1917 and the birth of the Soviet Union led to a significant wave of Russian immigration that lasted into the 1920s.

The people who came from Russia during this time differed from earlier Russian immigrants in a major way—many of them were not poor. Most of the Russian immigrants who had arrived several decades earlier had been either freed serfs or relatives of freed serfs. They had no money, no land, and usually no education. Most of the Russians who made up this new wave of immigration, however, were not former serfs. They were members of Russia's educated upper class, whose lands and businesses had been seized by the new Communist government.

In the Soviet Union, people from the wealthy and upper classes now feared for their lives. Their lands and their means of earning a living were taken away from them. If they spoke out against the new government's policies, they might be persecuted, exiled (forcibly sent) to Siberia,  or even killed. In the past, wealthy landowners had supported the czar. With the czar no longer in power, the future for these once-wealthy Russians was uncertain. Although it was not an easy decision to make, about 2 million Russians left their country during the Russian Revolution. Most of them settled in Europe, and about 30,000 immigrated to the United States.

Although once members of a privileged class in Russia, these new Russian immigrants faced many of the same challenges as the poorer serfs had before them. In the Soviet Union, many of these new immigrants had worked as professionals in the government and the legal system. They soon found that the training they had received in Russia did not qualify them for the same professions in the United States. Some Russian immigrants of this era used their experience in the upper class to take jobs in homes as maids or servants. Some who knew English found jobs as teachers. Still others had no choice but to toil away in factories, side by side with other Russian immigrants who were descended from serfs.

Many people in America, including Russian immigrants, watched with interest the changes taking place in Russia. Although many of the new Russian immigrants had left because of the new government, they now began to respect it. They saw many problems with the capitalist American economy, especially the way in which many business owners treated their employees. Many Russian immigrants thought that business owners valued their own interests above the welfare of their workers. Some Russian Americans believed that a socialist form of government, similar to that in the USSR, in which most businesses were owned by the government, was needed to reform American factories and farms. To promote these reforms, many Americans, including Russian Americans, joined the labor movement.

# The Labor Movement

Today, the United States has laws that protect workers. For example, laws specify a minimum wage, or the lowest amount of money a worker can earn per hour. In addition, workplaces must be safe, and there are laws that limit the employment of children under the age of 18. Many other laws also protect the rights and safety of workers.

During the Industrial Revolution—the period in the United States when the economy changed from one based on farming to one based mostly on manufacturing—such laws did not exist.

In the mid- to late 1800s, the United States was flooded with immigrants looking for jobs, and business owners were swamped with people who wanted to work. The owners, therefore, could pay as little money for as many hours of work as they thought necessary. If a worker chose to quit because of the low pay or unfair treatment, another immigrant was there to take the job.

When workers in the United States began to press for change and reform, the labor movement was born. People involved in the labor movement wanted better working conditions for laborers, including safer workplaces, limited working hours, and higher pay. They also believed that workers should get paid if they had been hurt on the job and were unable to work.

*Hundreds of union strikers demonstrate in Union Square in New York City in 1913. They carry signs in many languages representing the many immigrant groups living in New York.*

## Read All About It!

Many Russian-language newspapers sprang up in Russian immigrant communities around the United States. Some newspapers merely translated national and local news so Russians could be kept informed. Some newspapers published letters from their readers, describing their feelings about leaving their homeland and living in America. Still other newspapers published articles about government, socialism, and labor reform. It is estimated that during the 1920s, the three major Russian newspapers had about 75,000 subscribers combined. One of those newspapers—*Novoe russkoe slovo,* or *New Russian World*—still survives today. It began in 1910 and claims to be the oldest Russian-language newspaper in the world.

These ideas are common today, but during the late 1800s and early 1900s, many people considered them radical. Business owners were afraid that the government would agree with the laborers. Then the government might pass laws telling business owners how to operate their factories and treat their employees. America was supposed to be a free country, many business owners thought, in which they were allowed to run their businesses as they pleased. Government involvement would be a form of socialism, not capitalism.

People in the labor movement used several methods to get their message across. They held demonstrations at which they spoke passionately about their cause. They sent out flyers and newsletters, explaining their ideas to fellow workers, newspapers, and government officials. They also encouraged workers to go on strike, or leave their jobs until working conditions changed. After all, if there were no workers, there would be no businesses.

Thousands of Russian immigrants joined the cause. Many had been oppressed by the Russian czars and nobles. They felt that American business owners who treated their employees unfairly were comparable to the nobles who had mistreated the serfs. Other Russian immigrants who came during the years of the Russian Revolution believed that if the United States had a more socialist form of government, many of the injustices they saw in the American workplace would be eliminated. These radical ideas about labor, along with the emergence of the Communist Party in the Soviet Union, led to a period during which many Americans feared Communists, often people from Russia. This period is known as the Red Scare.

# The Red Scare

As the Russian Revolution continued and several thousand Russian immigrants entered the United States each year, many Americans became suspicious of anything Russian or Communist. The attorney general of the United States, A. Mitchell Palmer, believed, as he put it, that "communism was eating its way into the homes of American workmen." In 1919, Palmer received the support of the U.S. Congress to raid suspected Communist organizations in the United States. These raids became known as the Palmer Raids. During one raid in December 1919, 249 Russians were arrested. They were not U.S. citizens, but they were in the country legally. Even so, the U.S. government had all of them deported, or sent back to the Soviet Union.

Because the U.S. government seemed to believe that many Russians were Communists, Americans began to believe that Russians in general should be feared. These beliefs and fears led to the loss of many jobs for hard-working Russian immigrants. Even Russian Americans who were not immigrants themselves, but descendants of immigrants, soon found themselves unemployed. Some Russian Americans were forced to leave their homes.

In order to survive the Red Scare, many Russian immigrants tried to hide their backgrounds. Many changed their names to sound more "American" and even begin attending churches other than the Russian Orthodox Church.

The Red Scare lasted only for a short time, from about 1919 to 1920. Still, its effects lasted much longer. Americans never quite forgot their fears of communism, and Russian Americans never quite forgot that Russians in America were persecuted at this time.

In addition, new laws were

*This cartoon published during the Red Scare of 1919 shows suspected Bolsheviks and anarchists being driven from an American city.*

passed that limited the number of immigrants allowed to enter the United States. The Quota Act, passed in 1921, based the number of people of each immigrant group allowed to enter the United States each year on a percentage of the number of people of that immigrant group that were already in the country in 1910. In other words, if in 1910 there were 100,000 people of a certain immigrant group in the United States, the 1921 law allowed a certain percentage of that number to enter the country each year. Consequently, immigrant groups that had large populations in the United States by 1910, such as the German, Irish, and English, were allowed more immigrants per year than immigrant groups from eastern and southern Europe, including the Soviet Union, which had smaller populations in the United States in 1910. The number of immigrants allowed into the United States was even further restricted by the Immigration Act of 1924.

## Emma Goldman

Emma Goldman was one of those deported in the December 1919 Palmer Raid. Goldman was born in Lithuania (a nation later under the control of the Soviet Union) in 1869 and immigrated to the United States in 1885. She was considered an anarchist—a person who does not believe in any form of government. In 1893, Goldman was arrested in New York City and sent to prison for starting a riot. She was released from prison in 1894, at which time she went to Europe.

Goldman returned to the United States occasionally to hold lectures explaining her ideas. After she was deported to the Soviet Union in 1919, she became a supporter of the Communist government. However, she soon began speaking out against some of the government's policies, and the Soviet Union also forced her to leave. After living in England and Spain, Goldman eventually died in Toronto, Canada. Her autobiography, *Living My Life*, was published in 1931.

# New Restrictions, New War

Back home in the USSR, the Soviet people tried to adjust to the new Communist government. Under Joseph Stalin, the government passed laws that did not allow people in Russia to do much more than work. People were told where they could and could not live, what jobs they could and could not have, and where and when they could travel. With such limitations, emigration from the USSR slowed. Before the Communist regime, around the time of the Russian Revolution, millions of Russians had emigrated to the United States. Between 1930 and 1944, however, only a little more than 14,000 left the USSR to settle in the United States.

Then, in the late 1930s, a new threat loomed on the horizon in the USSR—Germany. Led by Adolf Hitler's Nazi Party, German armies began invading other European nations to conquer their lands. World War II (1939–1945) was the result. The USSR and the United States, along with Britain and other countries, fought as allies against Germany, Japan, and Italy. World War II devastated Europe and the Soviet Union and took hundreds of thousands of lives in battle. In addition, millions of people died in German concentration camps. Most of these were Jews. (The Nazis' systematic killing of the Jews during World War II is called the Holocaust.) After years of extreme hardship and devastation, the war ended in 1945. Nazi Germany was crushed, and the Allies were victorious.

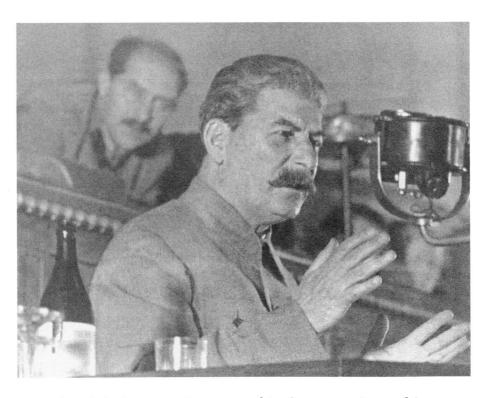

*Joseph Stalin, general secretary of the Communist Party of the Soviet Union, reports on the draft of a new Soviet constitution in the Kremlin in Moscow in 1936.*

The war left the Soviet Union in shambles. Many of its people, especially the Jews, had been forced from their homes. Others fled when the fighting came near. During the Battle of Stalingrad, which lasted from October 1942 to February 1943, about 500,000 soldiers in the Soviet Red Army lost their lives. This was more soldiers than the United States lost during the entire war. Some historians estimate that World War II reduced the Soviet population by about 25 million people. This number includes war casualties and refugees who fled the Soviet Union, some never to return.

## The Great Depression

While the Soviet Union was struggling with its new government, the United States was struggling with an economic catastrophe. At the end of 1929, the value of stocks fell dramatically. A stock is a unit of ownership that people can have in a company or business. Every stock has a specific money value. People can buy and sell their stocks in the stock market. In the 1920s, stocks were worth a lot of money. People wanted to buy stocks, so they took out loans to do so.

Then, in October 1929, the stock market "crashed," meaning that the prices of stocks fell. Many stocks that had been worth a lot of money were suddenly worthless. The people who owned those stocks, therefore, lost the money. People who had taken out loans to buy the stocks suddenly had no money to pay back those loans to the banks. This situation led to the Great Depression. During this time, businesses suffered and many people became poor, homeless, and hungry. Many immigrants, as well as other Americans, were in desperate need of jobs, but jobs were hard to find.

Some people, such as the family of Frederick Trutkoff, the son of Russian immigrants, survived by offering rooms for rent in their homes. Others offered to work for food. Eventually, the U.S. government stepped in and initiated plans to help people in need. Even so, it was a difficult time for most Americans.

# The Next Wave

When World War II ended, the United States, England, and the Soviet Union had to decide what to do with the millions of refugees left homeless by the war. Many of these refugees were from the Soviet Union. At first, the Soviet Union demanded that the refugees return to their country, and the United States and England agreed. But soon England and the United States changed their minds. They decided that Soviet refugees could choose to live where they wished.

Some refugees chose to return to the Soviet Union, but more than 100,000 chose not to. The United States offered these refugees a safe haven in America, and between 1947 and 1951, about 137,000 Soviet citizens were granted entry into the United States.

This latest wave of immigrants had many advantages that previous waves of immigrants did not. One of the most important was the support of the U.S. government. The United States had essentially invited the refugees to become Americans. Now the U.S. government set up programs to help them. The government helped the refugees

*This Russian immigrant family arrived in the United States in 1950. They lived in U.S. government–sponsored housing until the father found a job.*

obtain the documents necessary for entering the United States and set up classes for refugees to learn English. When the refugees finally arrived in America, the U.S. government helped them find jobs suited to their skills and training. With this aid, the immigrants were able to settle in areas throughout the United States, not just in major cities like New York, as previous immigrants had.

Many of the Russian immigrants who came to the United States during this period found work in the steel mills, factories, and mines of the Northeast. They often joined trade unions and lived in towns and neighborhoods close to their work. These neighborhoods were different from those in which earlier Russian immigrants settled. Russians often lived side by side with immigrants from countries such as Poland, Hungary, and Italy. As a result, they adopted American habits and language more quickly than their predecessors.

Joseph Stalin was not happy about the emigration of Soviet citizens to the United States. The United States was a capitalist society, and its values contrasted sharply with those of the Soviet Union. Stalin feared that Soviet citizens would want to emigrate if they heard about American ideals from their friends and relatives in the United States. As a result, Stalin passed new laws that made it almost impossible for Soviet citizens to travel outside the country.

The Soviet Union viewed the United States as a threat to communism. This new attitude toward the United States ushered in an era of tension between the two nations, and yet another wave of Russian immigration followed. ❖

Opposite: *These Jewish immigrants are shown on their journey from Russia in 1972 to their new home in Israel. They were among more than 100,000 Russian Jews who were allowed to leave the Soviet Union during the 1970s. Many of these immigrants came to the United States while others emmigrated to Israel.*

*Chapter Six*

# The Cold War

*1945–1991*

# The Iron Curtain

Winston Churchill was the prime minister, or leader, of Great Britain during World War II. In 1946, he said, "An iron curtain has descended across the continent." The term *iron curtain* referred to the invisible barrier that had begun to separate the capitalist countries of western Europe from the Communist countries of eastern Europe and Asia, primarily the Soviet Union.

After World War II, many eastern European countries, including Poland, Hungary, Yugoslavia, Czechoslovakia, and Romania, had become Communist under pressure from the Soviet Union. The position of these eastern European countries essentially formed a "curtain," separating the capitalist countries from the Communist countries. The Soviet Union also exerted its power over the Southeast Asian country of Korea, which adopted a Communist government. Meanwhile, Communists also came into power in China, the most populous nation in the world, and Vietnam.

The United States and western European countries feared the spread of communism. Likewise, the Soviet Union denounced European and American capitalism in favor of the USSR's Communist beliefs. This period in history is called the cold war.

# A Different Kind of War

The cold war between the United States and the Soviet Union was not a war in the traditional sense. No battles were fought. Instead, it was a war of competition and influence. The United States and the Soviet Union competed against each other to see which country could produce the greatest scientific achievements, the best scholars, the newest inventions, and the most weapons. Each country tried to spread its influence around the globe. The two nations were competing to be the most powerful nation in the world.

In 1945, during the last months of World War II, the United States unleashed one of the most destructive weapons of the modern era—the atomic bomb. Atomic bombs were dropped on the Japanese cities of Hiroshima and Nagasaki, killing or injuring nearly 200,000 people. (Many thousands more would die in the coming years, due to radiation poisoning from the bombs.) The use of these atomic bombs ended the war with Japan. At the same time, it demonstrated the devastating effect that one weapon could have.

In order to prove that it, too, was a military force to be feared, the Soviet Union began developing its own weapons and bombs. Both countries competed to develop weapons even more destructive than the atomic bomb. These were called thermonuclear weapons, or hydrogen bombs. Although none of these bombs were ever used in combat, it was known that if they were, their effects would be catastrophic. This so-called arms, or weapons, race between the United States and the Soviet Union continued throughout the next several decades.

# Life during the Cold War

The era of the cold war was not an easy time for Russian Americans. Many were suspected of having ties to the Soviet Union and the Communist Party. In the early 1950s, a U.S. senator named Joseph McCarthy claimed that the Department of State— the U.S. government branch that deals with foreign policy, or world issues—had been infiltrated by members of the Communist Party. The people he accused were not only politicians or Russian Americans but Americans from all walks of life. Many people whom McCarthy suspected of being Communists were called before congressional hearings to defend themselves. McCarthy's accusations were often based on very little fact, but the McCarthy hearings reinforced the country's fear of the Soviet Union. People's lives were ruined just by being accused, or named, even if they were never actually found to be guilty of anything.

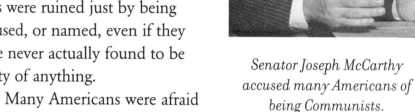

*Senator Joseph McCarthy accused many Americans of being Communists.*

Many Americans were afraid that the Soviet Union would attack the United States. They built bomb shelters below ground and stocked them with food and water supplies, in case of nuclear war. Schools held bomb drills, during which students practiced crouching under their desks for protection.

## TV Time

The television was invented in the United States—by a Russian immigrant. Vladimir Zworykin was born in 1889 in the town of Murom, Russia. He attended the Institute of Technology in St. Petersburg, Russia. In 1919, he immigrated to the United States and attended the University of Pennsylvania. A specialist in electronics, he became the director of the Electronic Research Laboratory at the Radio Corporation of America (RCA) in Princeton, New Jersey. Zworykin's research during the 1920s and 1930s helped develop the picture tube, an essential component of the television. He also helped invent television cameras. The development of television was put on hold during World War II. However, televisions were introduced to the public in 1946, and they quickly became very popular.

# The Race to Space

Another area in which the United States and the Soviet Union competed was the exploration of space. In the 1950s, both the United States and the Soviet Union experimented with various rockets and spacecraft that could go beyond Earth's atmosphere, go into orbit around the Earth, and survive space travel.

On October 4, 1957, the Soviet Union launched the first satellite, or spacecraft that orbited the earth. The size and shape of a large beach ball, it was called *Sputnik Zemli.* After 57 days in space, *Sputnik* tried to return to earth, but it was destroyed by the friction caused by the earth's atmosphere upon reentry.

A little more than a month later, the Soviets launched *Sputnik 2.* This time, the space capsule held a living creature, a dog named Laika. *Sputnik 2* and Laika traveled in space for nearly half a year—162 days. Laika died in space without oxygen, and *Sputnik 2* did not survive the return trip to Earth.

> ## It's a Fact!
>
> In Russian, the words *sputnik zemli* mean "traveling companion of the world." *Sputnik* was considered a companion of Earth as the planet traveled around the sun.

The United States was not far behind the USSR in efforts to travel into space. The United States launched its first satellite, *Explorer 1,* in January 1958 and its second, *Vanguard 2,* in March 1958. Several more satellites were launched by both countries over the next few years.

The next challenge was sending a human into space. Once again, the Soviet Union succeeded first. Yuri Gagarin became the first person to orbit Earth on April 12, 1961, in the spacecraft *Vostok 1.* But less than one month later, on May 5, 1962, the United States sent Alan Shepard into space.

The United States and the Soviet Union continued their competition in space travel. The United States was first in sending astronauts to the moon, in 1969, but the Soviet Union was first in creating a station in space. In 1995, almost 40 years after the Soviets' first spacecraft had been launched, the United States and Russia combined their efforts when the U.S. space shuttle *Atlantis* docked with the Russian space station *Mir.*

## It's a Fact!

The first woman in space was a Russian cosmonaut (*cosmonaut* is the Russian word for "astronaut"). Her name was Valentina Tereshkova, and her spacecraft left Earth on June 16, 1963. She orbited Earth 48 times. The United States would not send a woman astronaut into space until 1983—20 years later.

# An Identity Crisis

The decades of the cold war were confusing years for Russian Americans. Although they had left their homeland to begin a new life in America, they still felt loyal to their homeland and their Russian heritage. At the same time, many Russian Americans did not agree with the Communist Party or its form of government. Many were not sure if they should embrace their Russian culture in America or shun it for fear of being considered anti-American.

Despite these internal debates, many Russians who immigrated to the United States during this time found freedom in America that they did not have in the Soviet Union. Many Russian talents flourished in America's free and open society. One of these talented people was Bel Kaufman, who had arrived in America from Russia when she was 12 years old, in the early 1920s. In 1964, Kaufman's book *Up the Down Staircase* became a best seller, and it was later made into a movie. Her grandfather, Sholem Aleichem, who had immigrated to the United States before her in 1914, wrote the stories on which the Broadway musical *Fiddler on the Roof* was based.

Another notable Russian immigrant, Vladimir Nabokov, was born into an aristocratic Russian family in St. Petersburg in 1899. The family left Russia in 1917 during the Russian Revolution. After living in Europe for many years, Nabokov immigrated to the United States in 1940. One of his most popular novels was *Lolita*, which was published in 1955. Like Kaufman's *Up the Down Staircase*, it was also made into a movie.

Louise Berliawsky was also born in 1899, in Kiev, Russia. In 1905, her family came to the United States and settled in Maine. In 1920, she married Charles Nevelson, and she became known as Louise Nevelson. Louise Nevelson studied art and became a well-known and respected sculptor. Her first major art exhibit, called *Sixteen Americans*, was held at the Museum of Modern Art in New York City in 1959. Many more important exhibits of her work were to follow.

*Sculptor Louise (Berliawsky) Nevelson is shown in this photograph from 1973.*

An artist of a different sort, George Balanchine, was born in 1904 in St. Petersburg. He studied dance with the Imperial Ballet Academy there and traveled through Europe with a dance company called the Ballets Russes. Balanchine was invited by an American ballet lover, Lincoln Kirstein, to form a ballet company in the United States. With Kirstein, Balanchine began the American Ballet Company in 1935. Today, the

American Ballet Company is one of the premier dance companies in the United States.

Even though the United States and the Soviet Union were engaged in the cold war, Russian culture did not diminish in the United States in the decades after World War II. Russian Americans still attended Russian Orthodox churches and gathered at Russian meeting places, like Rova Farms in New Jersey. Russian immigrants and Americans who had Russian ancestors often married within the Russian community, keeping the Russian Orthodox faith and traditions alive.

# Russian Jews Leave the USSR

During the decades of the cold war, the Soviet government refused to let people leave the country. In the 1970s, however, the Soviet Union lifted its emigration restrictions for part of its population—the Jews.

In 1948, the nation of Israel had been established as a Jewish state. Many Jewish people who had been displaced during World War II made their way to Israel to start new lives. Jews who went to Israel came from many countries, including Russia.

Throughout the history of Russia and the Soviet Union, the government always tried to control its Jewish population. Under Stalin's leadership, many Jews were accused of conspiring with the United States and were arrested. Although persecution of Jews was not legal in the Soviet Union after World War II, many Jews still faced discrimination. They were often refused jobs, housing, and education.

Then, in 1971, the Soviet government decided that some Jews could leave Russia to be reunited with family members who lived in Israel or in other parts of the world. This decision came about for two reasons. First, many Russian Jews were pressuring the government into letting them leave. In February 1971, Russian Jews demonstrated in front of the Supreme Soviet building in Moscow. Some of the people who participated in the demonstration were allowed to leave the Soviet Union. Second, by lifting some restrictions on emigration and thus demonstrating its willingness to allow its citizens to travel outside the country, the Soviet Union was trying to improve its reputation with the United States.

As a result, many Soviet Jews left the USSR in the 1970s, and it is estimated that more than 100,000 settled in the United States. This large movement of Russian Jews from the Soviet Union is sometimes called the Russian Diaspora. (The term *diaspora* usually refers to the displacement of the Jews throughout history.) Many of these immigrants settled in Jewish communities in New York City, such as Brighton Beach in Brooklyn. This area is sometimes referred to as "Little Odessa," after a Russian seaport.

Other Russian Jews who left the USSR in the 1970s established a community in San Francisco, California. Other Russian communities also flourish in the San Francisco Bay Area. One is made up of earlier immigrants and their descendants who practice the Russian Orthodox faith. Another consists mostly of wealthy recent immigrant men in their 20s and 30s.

For more than 60 years, Russian immigrants in San Francisco have supported a Russian cultural center, called simply the Russian Center. As the center explains on its Web site:

*The Russian Center of San Francisco was founded in 1939 by Russian immigrants as a focal point for the preservation of their rich cultural heritage. Tradition was passionately kept alive through operas, operettas, choirs, grand balls, folk dance, ensembles and plays. Generation followed generation, and still the goal remains to preserve and display the warmth and spirit of the Russian culture.*

# An Easier Journey

The journey for Russian immigrants in the 1960s and 1970s was far less difficult than it had been for the Russians who immigrated to the United States in previous decades. Travel by airplane replaced travel by train and ship. Immigrants no longer had to pass through Ellis Island in order to gain entry to the country. Russian churches and clubs that had been established for decades helped the new immigrants meet people and adjust to American life.

*A group of Jewish immigrants is greeted with flowers as they arrive from the Soviet Union in 1972. They were among a large group of Russian Jews who were allowed to emmigrate to other countries, including the United States, during the 1970s.*

In addition, many immigrants during this time had family or friends already living in the United States. These contacts made the transition much easier than in previous decades. One aspect of immigration became more difficult, however. Each immigrant needed more formal paperwork and documentation, such as visas, than had been necessary before.

## Israel, Long Ago and Today

Israel is an ancient land, and Jews lived there thousands of years ago. In 586 B.C., a Babylonian king named Nebuchadnezzar forced the Jews to leave Israel and settle in the ancient city of Babylon to the east. The settling of the Jews outside of Israel is called the Jewish Diaspora. Throughout history, Jews were continually being displaced from their homelands by one ruler or another. When Jews left Russia and other parts of Europe during World War II, and later during the 1970s, their new homelands became part of the Jewish Diaspora. In 1948, Israel was formerly declared a Jewish state by the United Nations. The Palestinians whose ancestors had lived in Israel for centuries dispute the Jews' claims to the land. This dispute has led to the struggle today between Jewish people and Palestinian people in Israel and the land known as the Gaza Strip.

# Without Permission

Not every Russian immigrant who came to the United States in the 1970s did so with permission from the Soviet government. Some Russians defected—they left the Soviet Union and decided to seek asylum in the United States. Having asylum meant that the defectors were protected by the U.S. government and that the Soviet government could not force them to return to the USSR.

One person who defected during the 1970s was a Russian ballet dancer named Mikhail Baryshnikov. He was born in 1948 in Latvia, a nation that at the time was controlled by the Soviet Union. After studying dance in Leningrad, Baryshnikov joined the Kirov Ballet in 1967. In 1974, he toured with the Bolshoi Ballet in Canada. Instead of returning with the ballet company to the Soviet Union, however, Baryshnikov left the company and entered the United States. There, he danced with the American Ballet Company—the group that fellow Russian immigrant George Balanchine helped establish in 1935.

At this point during the cold war, many Americans supported people who left the Soviet Union to live in the United States. Americans saw these defections as an affirmation of the American way of life. Defecting, after all, was not only a difficult but a dangerous decision. Defectors who were caught by Soviet authorities faced not only imprisonment, but most likely death. So people's willingness to risk such danger in order to leave the Soviet Union and live in the United States seemed to show that life was better in the United States.

Tension remained between the United States and the Soviet Union through the 1980s. It was not until the fall of the Communist Party and the dissolution of the USSR in 1991 that the borders of the Soviet Union were once again open for emigration.

Opposite: *Russian gymnast Olga Korbut (center) won three gold medals at the 1972 Olympics in Munich, Germany. Korbut immigrated to the United States in 1991 and lives in Scottsdale, Arizona with her husband and son where she runs a gymnastics school.*

*Chapter Seven*

# The Iron Curtain Lifts

*1991–Today*

# The Beginning of the End

The Russian word *perestroika* means "rebuilding," and the word *glasnost* means "openness." These two words symbolized a movement begun in the Soviet Union by Soviet leader Mikhail Gorbachev in the mid-1980s. Gorbachev hoped to improve the Soviet Union through rebuilding the economy and being more open with Soviet citizens about the Soviet government and the Communist Party.

Gorbachev's promotion of perestroika and glasnost, however well-intentioned, did not have the positive effect he had hoped for. Prices on products sold to the people of Russia went up, and people could no longer afford to buy things.

*Most Russian immigrants have settled
in these states.*

Russians also learned about the unfair ways in which the Soviet Union had treated and repressed its citizens over the years. They were not satisfied with perestroika and glasnost only. They wanted a better way of life. They wanted an end to communism.

# Russia Once More

The country of Russia had never totally disappeared from the landscape of the Soviet Union. During the era of the Soviet Union, Russia had been called the Russian Republic, and it had its own governing body. One of the members of the Russian Republic's government was Boris Yeltsin. Under Yeltsin's leadership, the Russian Republic declared its independence from the Soviet Union on June 11, 1990. By declaring its independence, the Russian Republic reflected the hopes of many that the Soviet Union would disband and that Communist rule would end.

Other republics within the Soviet Union began to declare their independence, too. Although Gorbachev tried to stop these uprisings, he failed, and eventually Yeltsin gained control. Gorbachev officially resigned as leader of the Soviet Union on December 25, 1991. In a free election—the first such election that Russia had ever had—Boris Yeltsin was elected the president of the Russian Federation. The Soviet Union no longer existed, and the Communist Party no longer ruled in Russia.

*Former Soviet president Mikhail Gorbachev is the founder of the Gorbachev Foundation of North America, which is dedicated to the spread of democracy.*

Despite these changes, Russia still faced an old problem—a struggling economy. As the new economy tried to find its way, some Russians once again began looking to the United States as a place where earning a living would be easier.

# Russian Americans Today

"I was too young to be involved in the decision-making process," says Evgeniya Dymtchenko, "but I would say that my parents wanted to come [to the United States] because this country offers so many more opportunities to live a good life."

Dymtchenko and her parents were among the approximately 400,000 Russians who immigrated to the United States between 1990 and 1998. Dymtchenko arrived in the United States in 1991, at the age of 10. Her parents had friends and relatives in the United States, making their decision to emigrate a bit easier.

As Dymtchenko recalls, assimilating was not easy. "In the beginning, going to school was definitely the hardest to get used to," she explains. "I didn't speak any English, and not being able to make new friends was very tough." Back in Russia, she had lived "in a big city where there were always people around, and you could just walk places instead of having to drive, and there was always something to do," Dymtchenko continues. "Now I·live in suburbia [in New Jersey], and there is not much to do nearby."

Besides the city where she was born, Dymtchenko admits to missing other things about Russia, too. "What I miss most about Russia is my family because everyone except for my parents is still over there. I also miss the food . . . everything just tastes so delicious over there."

During the years of the cold war, many Russian Americans chose not to reveal their heritage. Some of them feared a negative reaction from neighbors, coworkers, or even the government. They feared they might be accused of being Communists and a threat to the United States. Today, however, many Russian Americans, especially those who immigrated in the 1990s, embrace their heritage. "I try to preserve my Russian roots by speaking, reading, and writing the Russian language," says Dymtchenko. "My family and I also celebrate Russian holidays and observe certain Russian traditions. I also enjoy eating Russian foods."

Dymtchenko is also able to enjoy one more freedom that previous Russian immigrants did not have. "Most importantly," she says, "I have gone to Russia every year for the last six years, and I plan on keeping that tradition for as long as I can."

In contrast to most of those who came in the past, today's Russian immigrants do not necessarily settle only in New York City's Brighton Beach or Lower East Side. Instead, they live throughout the United States. In fact, Russian immigrants have settled as far north as Minnesota and as far south as Arizona and Florida.

In 2000, the U.S. Census (an official count of the U.S. population done every ten years) revealed that nearly 3 million people claim to have Russian ancestors or to be from Russia. The state with the most Russian Americans

> ## It's a Fact!
>
> **According to the 2000 U.S. Census, 2,652,214 people living in the United States claim to have Russian ancestors. That equals slightly less than 1 percent of the total U.S. population. In addition, the census counted 340,177 people who immigrated from Russia and now live in the United States.**

is still New York, with about 460,000. California is close behind, with 402,480. The states with the next-highest Russian-American populations are Florida (201,559), New Jersey (189,524), and Pennsylvania (178,855). Russian Americans live in every state.

Compared to Russian immigrants in past decades, who were mostly unskilled laborers, the U.S. Citizenship and Immigration Service reports that 10 percent of all Russian immigrants since 2001 seek jobs as professionals or in technical occupations. However, some immigrants who were doctors or lawyers in their homeland find it difficult to work in their professions in the United States. Since their training is often somewhat different from that of similar professionals in America, they may have to return to school or study on their own before they are allowed to practice law or medicine. These immigrants often obtain lower-paying jobs while they study. Immigrants with technical training find it easier to adapt their skills to American industry.

*Two residents of the Russian community of Brighton Beach in Brooklyn, New York, meet in front of a Russian grocery store in 2002.*

Children make up a significant number of new immigrants from Russia. Some children come to America with their families while others are adopted by U.S. citizens. In 2001, more than 4,000 Russian children were adopted by American families. This number is second only to the number of children adopted from China each year. These children range in age from a few months to fifteen years old. Russian children who are legally adopted by U.S. citizens gain U.S. citizenship when the adoption process is complete and they enter the United States with their adoptive parents. In this way, they become instant Americans.

# The Impact of Russian Americans

Russian Americans and Russian culture have had an enriching influence on the United States. These influences date from every era of Russian immigration, from the Russian fur traders who settled in Alaska to the Russian factory workers during the Industrial Revolution and the Russian scientists and artists whose skills and talents enrich every aspect of American life in the 21st century.

Some Russian foods, for instance, have become part of American cuisine. Borscht is a traditional Russian soup made from beets. Beef Stroganoff is a popular dish of thinly sliced beef in a sour cream sauce that was created in St. Petersburg in the 1890s and named after a noble Russian family, the Stroganovs. Blintzes, a traditional Russian dish, are thin pancakes rolled around a fruit or cheese filling.

Russian cultural influences can also be found in art. Fabergé eggs are one such art form that originated in Russia. In 1884, Czar Alexander III asked a well-known jewelry maker,

Peter Carl Fabergé, to create a special gift for the czarina (the wife of the czar). Fabergé created a beautiful egg decorated with gold and jewels. Other jewelers have continued the art of making intricately decorated eggs for the Fabergé company. Today they are still called Fabergé eggs.

Another traditional craft from Russia is wooden nesting dolls, known as *matryoshka* dolls. What makes these dolls special is that one doll fits inside another. Inside the largest doll snugly sits a smaller doll. Inside this doll is an even smaller doll, and so on. The dolls are usually given as gifts for birthdays or at Christmastime. Although the dolls were originally produced as toys, they have become a symbol of Russian culture and are collected by many people around the world.

Since the end of the cold war, Russians have made significant contributions in American sports. Russian hockey players such as Sergei Federov, currently of the Anaheim Mighty Ducks, have been stars on American teams. Anna Kournikova, who lives in Miami, Florida, is one of the world's most recognized tennis players.

# Looking Back and Forward

Frederick Trutkoff stands on the shore of the lake at Rova Farms and reminisces. "The lake had a floating dock," Trutkoff recalls. "The guys would lie on the dock in the middle of the lake, and invite the girls over. We were just American kids, having fun." They were "American kids," but they all had Russian backgrounds.

"I think everything happens for a reason," Trutkoff reflects:

*If my mother and father hadn't chosen to come to the United States, I would not have been American. I was the first person in my family to ever go to college. I served in the United States Army during the Korean War. I had a good job working for the federal government, which allowed me to buy a house and raise a family.*

Today, Trutkoff is retired and lives in Manchester Township, New Jersey, with his wife, Sigrid. Manchester Township is only a few miles from Rova Farms. "It's strange, isn't it?" he says. "When I was a kid, I used to spend summers here. And now that I'm retired, I live only a few miles away."

In part, Trutkoff credits the strength and courage of his parents, who made the arduous journey to the United States, for his success in life. "I can't say it enough. Everything happens for a reason," he concludes.

Frederick Trutkoff never lived in Russia, nor has he ever visited there, so he does not know what his parents left behind. Twenty-three-year-old Evgeniya Dymtchenko did live in Russia, and although she makes frequent trips to visit her homeland, she is grateful to live in the United States. "I love the fact that this country has given me the chance to do what I want and to be who I want," says Dymtchenko. "I like knowing that in this country, if I work hard and do my best, I will be rewarded for it in the sense that I can shape my own future and build the kind of life that I want."

Dymtchenko's words echo the sentiments of the millions of Russian immigrants who have ventured to the United States with the hopes of a better future.

# Time Line of Russian Immigration

| | |
|---|---|
| **1480** | Ivan the Great becomes the first czar of Russia; he sends the first expeditions into North America. |
| **1648** | A man from Siberia named Semyon Ivanov Dezhnyov sails through the narrow body of water that separates Asia from North America. |
| **1682** | Peter the Great becomes the czar of Russia; during his reign, he orders an expedition to North America. |
| **1728** | Danish sea captain Vitus Bering explores the strait separating Russia from North America at the request of Russian czar Peter the Great. |
| **1741** | Bering lands in North America on Kayak Island near Cape Saint Elias, Alaska. |
| **1745** | The first Russian fur trader in the Americas, Mikhail Nevodchikov, lands on an island of Alaska's Aleutian islands. |
| **1784** | The first permanent Russia settlement in America is established on Kodiak Island, Alaska, by Grigory Ivanovich Shelikhov. |
| **1794** | A Russian Orthodox church is built on Kodiak Island. |
| **1804** | The Russian-American Company establishes the first settlement on Alaska's mainland: Novo-Arkhangel'sk, later renamed Sitka. |
| **1808** | Sitka becomes the capital of Russian America. |
| **1811** | The first Russian settlement is established in California: Fort Ross. |
| **1817** | The Russians and the Kashaya Indians of California sign a deed for the lands on which Fort Ross was built. |
| **1842** | Russians leave Fort Ross. |
| **1861** | In Russia, more than 20 million serfs are granted their freedom. |
| **1867** | Russia sells Alaska to the United States. |

**1880–1930** More than 3 million people come to the United States from Russia.

**1881** In Russia, Czar Alexander II is assassinated; life becomes more difficult in Russia; the first pogrom against Russian Jews is conducted in Russia.

**1892** Ellis Island becomes the main port of entry for most immigrants to the United States.

**1914–1918** World War I is fought; millions of Russian soldiers die during the war.

**1917–1921** The Russian Revolution is fought; Czar Nicholas II steps down as czar in 1917; he is the last czar of Russia.

**1922** Russia becomes the Union of Soviet Socialist Republics, or the USSR; the government is controlled by the Communist Party.

**1939–1945** World War II is fought; thousands of people are left homeless, including Jews, Russian Jews, and Russians.

**1945–1991** The cold war between the United States and the Soviet Union results in severe restrictions on emigration from the USSR.

**1970s** The Soviet Union allows Jews to emigrate, but not the general population of the Soviet Union.

**1990–1998** About 400,000 Russians immigrate to the United States as the Soviet Union and the Communist Party slowly dissolve.

**1991** The last leader of the Communist Party, Mikhail Gorbachev, resigns. Boris Yeltsin is elected the first president of the Russian Federation.

**1995** In June, the U.S. space shuttle *Atlantis* docks with the Russian space station *Mir*.

**1999** Boris Yeltsin resigns as president of the Russian Federation.

**2000** Vladimir Putin is elected president of the Russian Federation.

**2001** The United States is attacked by terrorists on September 11. Putin declares that Russia will help in the fight against terrorism.

**2003** Russian immigrant Shlema Livshits becomes one of the oldest people in history to take the Oath of Citizenship at age 104.

# Glossary

**assimilate**  To absorb into a culture or tradition.

**asylum**  A place of refuge; protection given people who chose to leave another country.

**autocracy**  A form of government in which one person or group has unlimited power.

**culture**  The language, arts, traditions, and beliefs of a society.

**democracy**  Government by the majority rule of the people.

**emigrate**  To leave a place in order to settle somewhere else.

**ethnic**  Having certain racial, national, tribal, religious, or cultural origins.

**exile**  To force someone out of a country because of the person's beliefs or actions; a person forced to leave his or her country.

**immigrate**  To come into a foreign country in order to live there permanently.

**iron curtain**  A political barrier that isolated Soviet-controlled countries from the rest of the world.

**pogrom**  An organized massacre in Russia, usually of Jewish people.

**prejudice**  Negative opinion formed without just cause.

**refugee**  Someone who flees for safety reasons, especially to another country.

**socialism**  An economic system in which the government owns some businesses but not all.

# Further Reading

## BOOKS

Bowen, Richard A. *The Russian Americans: We Came to America.*
Philadelphia: Mason Crest Publishers, 2003.

Frost, Helen. *Russian Immigrants, 1860–1915.* Mankato, Minn.:
Capstone Books, Blue Earth Books, 2003.

Malvasi, Meg Green. *The Russian Americans: Immigrants in America.*
San Diego: Gale Group, Lucent Books, 2002.

Peterson, Tiffany. *We Are America: Russian Americans.* Chicago:
Heinemann Library, 2003.

## WEB SITES

California State Military Museum. "Historic California Posts: Fort Ross
(Fort Rossiya)." http://www.militarymuseum.org/FtRoss.html.
Downloaded on September 9, 2004.

Congress of Russian Americans. URL: http://www.russian-americans.org.
Downloaded on September 9, 2001.

EuroAmericans.net. "Russians in America." URL: http://www.euro-
americans.net/russians.htm. Downloaded on September 9, 2004.

The Lower East Side Tenement Museum. URL: http://www.tenement.org.
Downloaded on September 9, 2004.

# Index